RASPBERRY PI

*A complete guide to start learning RaspberryPi on your own. Learn an **easy** way to setup and build your projects, avoid common mistakes, and develop solid skills in computer technology.*

Michail Kölling

CODING
HOOD

Table of Contents

Introduction

We can find a lot of different programming languages to work with to write codes and a lot of tools and accessories that sneak in and help us get things done as well. With all this technology growing and changing all the time, sometimes, this is going to make beginners feel like they are too far behind and that they should just give up rather than trying. They worry that the work is going to be too hard for them to get it done. The neat thing here is that Raspberry Pi is going to be there to help to solve this problem. This is a small computer board, which is about the size of a credit card, that can hook up to the computer monitor or your TV.

To start, the Raspberry Pi device is going to be anything that we would expect our traditional desktop computer to do, such as processing different voices, looking online, creating tables, doing gaming, playing videos in HD, and more. Even more than this, we will find that this device also comes with the ability to interact with the world outside as well.

As you can see, there is quite a bit that we need to know when it is time to work with Raspberry Pi, and you will be able to utilize it for a lot of the different projects that are out there.

The following chapters will discuss the Raspberry Pi. The Raspberry Pi is increasingly popular. Why, though? What's all the fuss about? So many people are interested in this amazing little microcomputer and all of the things that it can do. This book will focus on all of the reasons that people are falling in love with the Raspberry Pi and its various capabilities. We'll also be learning how to program in Python and the plethora of different things that you can use the Raspberry Pi for.

We will look at some options that are out there for this device, and we will learn some coding that is necessary to get it started. It is such a simple device that we can work with, but it does make the difference when it comes to how well we can learn about and work with computers and even how we can work through the process of learning new coding and programming language.

If you take a look at the structure of the Raspberry Pi, the first thing you'll notice is how small it is. The size of a Raspberry Pi is similar to that of a typical credit card. This small form-factor of the Raspberry Pi is itself a characteristic feature of the device, although it may not look entirely like a final product straight out of the box. When compared to the modern PC motherboards, the Raspberry Pi is a computer that has been made available to the general consumer in a tiny form-factor, low price tag, and functionality, which you would normally expect from a full-sized Personal Computer. Owing to such characteristics, the Raspberry Pi is suitable for a wide range of purposes. Browsing the internet, playing modest video games, interacting with popular social media channels, the perfect system to learn programming and coding, all the way to using the Raspberry

Pi in innovative and creative projects building devices such as retro emulator in variety of forms and controlling and handling complex circuits. The Raspberry Pi does not have one specific use, in reality; it's the complete opposite; in the sense that the limitations of the Raspberry Pi are in actuality the limitations of one's imagination regarding the projects in which this device can be used.

Moreover, there's an entire Raspberry Pi community on the internet dedicated to helping out people in their queries regarding the device. Whether you bought your first Raspberry Pi and need help setting it up or if you're using a Raspberry Pi in a project, you will be surprised at how positively and quickly the community joins the discussion forums and give their suggestions and feedback to your questions.

The birth of Raspberry Pi was inspired by the notion that fully functioning computers in a compact size made available to the general consumer at a plausible price would hold enough power as to not only facilitate the educational industry but also making computer technology easy to implement and customize in various projects (educational projects, DIY projects or any experiment that can use the prowess of the Raspberry Pi); in short, the prospects are virtually unlimited). The Raspberry Pi Foundations was established in 2012, and after a limited production of units, the beta testing became a huge success and today, Raspberry Pi is the leading device which has taken a strong foothold in various human interactive environments including homes, offices, smart factories, data centers, interactive classrooms and other such places which can take advantage of the features of a small handheld computer.

When we think about computers, we usually find a monitor, a keyboard, a mouse, and a CPU. But the Raspberry Pi is a fully functional computer system that is embedded into a small single credit-card-sized board and costs less than most of the video games you'll find. With it, people will be able to do a variety of things such as building robots, learning how to code, and an assortment of other fascinating and strange projects.

Society needs programmers now more than ever before, and the release of the Raspberry Pi has echoed a brand-new love for computer technology and science.

The Raspberry Pi might not be a great choice for primary PC with its 512 MB to 1 GB of RAM and for storage purposes, an SD card, but it can even be used for several other reasons from giving power to robots made from home and developing retro video games to becoming home theater PCs and to online-connected weather stations.

If you're searching for motivation to begin your very own Raspberry Pi venture, at that point, you've gone to the perfect spot since we have arranged probably the best use cases around to give you a few thoughts.

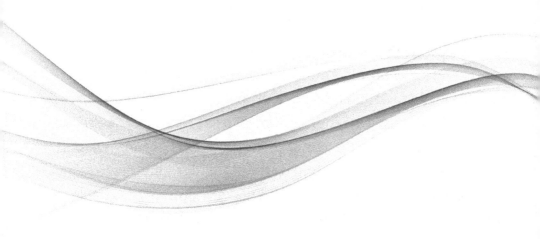

Chapter 1

Basics of raspberry PI

What is Raspberry Pi?

Raspberry Pi is a low-cost single computer developed by Raspberry Pi Foundation, a charity based in UK. The Raspberry Pi can be connected to a monitor or television and can be operated using a USB mouse and keyboard. The dimension of the device is comparable to that of a credit card and requires low operating power. It comprises all the commonly available interfaces used in general purposes computers such as USB ports, audio ports, HDMI output port, ethernet ports, etc. In addition to these standard interfaces, some general-purpose input/output(GPIO) ports are also available in this device. These GPIO pins can be configured to act either as an input or as an output port, thereby making the device to function as a low power high performance embedded system. There are several versions of the Raspberry Pi available in the market, depending on the features provided.

The Raspberry Pi Foundation developed the Raspberry Pi in England, and the first device was launched in early 2012. To this date, many versions of the Raspberry Pi have been released and have continuously improved with each version.

There are even industrial models and versions that have become smaller and smaller, such as the Raspberry Pi Zero. By the end of 2017, more than 17 million Raspberry Pi units had already been sold.

The goal of the Development

The goal of the Raspberry Pi Foundation is to introduce young people to hardware and software programming and to facilitate their entry into programming.

The Raspberry Pi is relatively inexpensive to buy, and therefore the entry barriers to development with the Raspberry Pi are very low. The unique thing about the Raspberry Pi is that this small credit card format hides a full-fledged computer.

In the meantime, numerous projects for everyday and professional life can be implemented very easily. The Raspberry Pi Foundation also plays an important role here. On the website raspberrypi.org, you can find numerous suggestions for very ambitious projects, which can be easily rebuilt.

The Raspberry Pi Foundation also carries out numerous school projects to introduce young students into programming. Since there are many different kinds of software and hardware-based on Raspberry Pi projects out there, I would like to showcase some of them in the next chapter.

So much can be said in advance, as there are now entire business models and commercial devices based on a Raspberry Pi. This already shows that the Raspberry Pi has become very widespread and is no longer just a learning device for young people.

Hardware Specifications

Your Raspberry Pi has the following hardware specifications:

BCM2837B0 Chip

Quad-core 64-bit ARM cortex A53 CPU

Clocked at 1.4GHz

Cypress 43455 chip for wireless and Bluetooth

400 MHz Video Core IV GPU

1 GB LPDDR22-900 SDRAM

802.11 ac Wireless LAN

Bluetooth 4.2 chip

Power

Micro-usb power in

2.5 Amp supply recommended

PoE Connector Added

Browsing the internet

You can connect you Raspberry Pi to the internet either by Ethernet cable or wireless connection. To connect to wi-fi, look at the top right side of the screen. You will see an icon with a red cross. Select the correct network from the drop-down menu. Provide the password for your wi-fi connection, and your Raspberry Pi is connected to the internet.

What is Raspberry Pi meant for?

A Raspberry Pi laptop can be used like any other Linux based system. The "hard disk drive" of this system is small – instead of a traditional hard disk, it uses a micro SD card. You can easily work on your office documents, run games, and play videos.

You can connect to the command line interface of the Raspberry Pi using Secure Socket Shell (SSH) from any computer. SSH is a network protocol that supplies administrators with a secure manner to access a remote computer. In such a scenario, you will not get a graphical interface from the connection. You WILL, however, be able to execute commands from the terminal application on another computer. The commands will execute through the SSH onto your Raspberry Pi.

If there is a requirement to access the raspberry pi remotely and you require a graphical interface as well, you can do so with the help of virtual network computing. This would be a slow affair but would allow you to connect visually to your Raspberry Pi if you needed to.

What is required along with the Raspberry Pi 3b+ model

For the Raspberry Pi to work fully as a desktop computer, you will require the following equipment to attach to the ports and connections listed earlier:

•*Power supply*: You would require a USB-A to micro-USB lead. A 5.1-volt micro USB supply powers it. The best choice would be to buy a 300-watt power supply from your local retailer. This would provide enough power to your Raspberry Pi to allow you to work on it with no further upgrades. Make sure that you do not overload the power supply. Take a close look at the specifications provided on the power supply to give you a fair idea of the power handling capacity of the system.

•*Keyboard and Mouse*: Raspberry Pi allows you to connect to any USB or wireless keyboard or mouse. The unit comes with 4 USB ports, down to two free USB ports after connecting the keyboard and mouse.

•*Monitor*: The original Raspberry Pi supported HDMI and RCA ports. Raspberry Pi 3 has HDMI and magic 3.5mm media ports. Every version of Raspberry Pi is HDMI compatible, meaning that you can easily connect it to your home HDMI–compatible TV.

•*Micro SD card*: If you want to use your own micro-SD card in your Raspberry Pi, you will have to get the NOOBS installer. NOOBS stands for "New Out Of the Box Software". This can be a relatively complicated process, so buying a prepared micro SD card is recommended. Prepared micro SD cards are not expensive and are likely to save you a lot of time, money, and headache. If you insist on preparing your own SD card, go to www.raspberrypi.org/downloads. While preparing your card, you can opt for a wide range of operating systems distributions, which can be a great advantage. If you are a new user to Linux; however, it is best to go for the NOOBS installer and use the standard Raspbian operating system it has to offer.

•*Case*: Your Raspberry Pi is only a motherboard. It does not have an enclosure. This is the reason it is priced so low. It is recommended that you purchase a case for the unit to protect it from wear and tear and prolong the duration of its life.

Booting from NOOBS

If you purchase a Raspberry Pi with a micro SD card containing NOOBS preinstalled, your setup will be much easier. After connecting to the monitor, it will show that the installer has been loaded. Click on "Install" and installation will be completed in a short time.

Raspberry Pi provides a Linux desktop that you can use like any other PC. It is easy to use and navigate if you are familiar with Windows environments.

Now that your Raspberry Pi is fully installed and configured, we can start exploring it in more detail. Get ready to dive in!

Accessories

Camera: back in 2013, the Raspberry Pi Foundation and its distributors were able to release the firmware update that would allow for a camera to be used with the Raspberry Pi. The camera is a flat cable that you can plug into the CSI connector. When you are looking at Raspbian, you are going to have to make sure that you enable the camera to run on the board through configuring the camera option. The Raspberry Pi camera can take up to a 1080p photo or shoot a 640 x 480p video. Three years later, the 8 megaPixels was released to the public.

Gertboard: the foundation made this accessory for educational purposes only so that the GPIO Pins were able to be expanded so that the interface could be controlled with a series of switches and sensors.

Infrared camera: this camera was going to be part of the camera module that would not contain the infrared filter, and it is known as the Pi NoIR.

Software

Operating system

As mentioned earlier, you are going to want to try and stick to the Raspbian operating system, which is an extension of Linux. There are other operating systems that you can use if you do not want to work with a Linux based operating system.

Driver APIs

The video-core iv for the graphics processor is going to be using a binary blob in which you will be able to prime into the graphics processing unit from an SD card and then only adding in the additional software when it has booted up. Most of the work that is done with the driver is going to be done with a closed source for the graphics processor and its related code. Any software use calls are going to run their code closed source, but there are specific applications that you can download to open the driver of origin that is inside of the kernel. The kernel's API is going to be designed for these closed libraries to make sure that the Pi is processing correctly, and the code is not being messed with, which could end up causing the Pi not to operate properly.

Firmware

All of the firmware that the Raspberry Pi uses is going to be closed sourced and use a binary blob that is freely redistributable. You are not going to find a lot of firmware that is going to be open source for the Pi.

Chapter 2

Setup

Setting Up Your Raspberry Pi

In this chapter, we're going to outline everything that you have to do to set up your Raspberry Pi. This will include everything that you need to get it up and running, so pay close attention. It is difficult at first, but it only gets easier from here! This guide assumes that you're working with a Raspberry Pi Model 3 B, the most recent model. However, if you're working with an older model, things will remain largely the same throughout the process.

First off, here's what you're going to need to set up your Pi so that it runs as a desktop computer:

- Monitor (obviously)
- Keyboard and mouse
- MicroSD card
- Operating system
- Choosing an Operating System

What operating system should you use on your Raspberry Pi? There are many different answers to this question. Many different companies have made versions of the operating systems that can run on the Raspberry Pi's software. Even Microsoft has released a version of Windows that can run on the hardware of the Raspberry Pi. So, bearing all of this in mind, what software specifically should you use on your Raspberry Pi?

Regardless of what operating system you want to use, NOOBS will offer support for it and is an excellent operating system installer. While I would recommend that you install Raspbian, ultimately, you have autonomy over whatever you decide to install on your Pi. Let's now talk about the setup process.

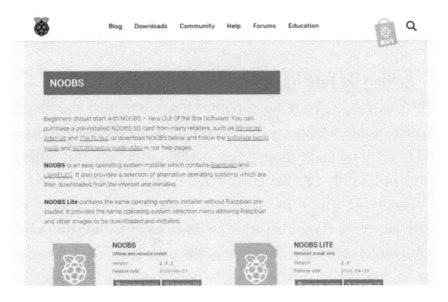

Installing NOOBS

These instructions will tell you how to set up Raspbian only. If you decide to install a different operating system, then this book will not be able to help you with that. However, as long as the installation is through NOOBS, the process should be the same for all operating systems. Therefore, you shouldn't have any problems installing them. With that said, let's install NOOBS first.

To set up your Raspberry Pi with an operating system, you will need to grab your SD card and insert it into your computer.

Search for SD Formatter 4.0. Download and install it. (Kindle formatting doesn't play nice with links, so I cannot link you, unfortunately.) It's released by an organization called the SD Association, so as long as you're getting it off their website, you should be in the clear.

Install the software and start up the SD Formatter program. Select your SD card's disk drive and then format it exactly as the default settings indicate.

Go to your download of the NOOBS installer. You can get it by searching for NOOBS and then heading to the link hosted by the Raspberry Pi organization.

Extract the files somewhere, such as your desktop. Copy the files that were extracted over to your SD card, and then you're set.

Take out the SD card and put it in your Raspberry Pi's SD card slot. Plug-in everything: your monitor via the HDMI port, your keyboard, and your mouse. Ensure that your monitor is on the right setting.

If all goes well, you should be clear to finally plug your Raspberry Pi into the wall and get to some heavy development. If you're using a newer Pi model, it should have built-in WiFi. Older models, however, will require you to connect to the internet via Ethernet or to plug in a WiFi adapter that is compatible with the Raspberry Pi. You'll know your Raspberry Pi is on when the indicator link on the Raspberry Pi is blinking. At this point, you'll know if everything is going well because the indicator light will be on, and you should have video displaying on your monitor.

Installing Raspbian

Now that we've installed NOOBS, we can proceed with installing Raspbian or your operating system of choice. Again, this book will only discuss Raspbian. Still, the process of installing the operating system is the same for all other operating systems that you can use for the Raspberry Pi.

On the main screen upon the operating system powering up, ensure that Raspbian is selected. This is the recommended operating system across most communities, especially for people who are new to Raspberry Pi.

Click Install next and then click Yes to confirm that it's going to overwrite your SD card.

Wait, and after a bit, your operating system will be installed. It's a straightforward process like I said.

Your Pi will reboot, and you'll be brought to the main screen for the Raspbian operating system.

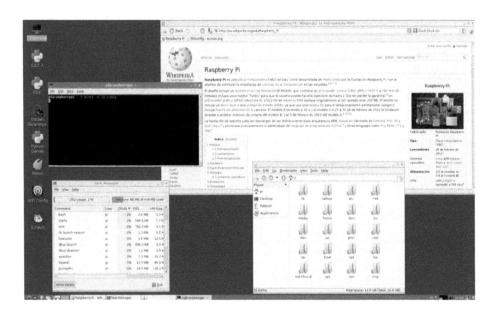

Getting Started

Now that you're on Raspbian's main screen, it's time to make the magic happen. This is where your adventures with the Raspberry Pi begin. Feel free to poke around a little bit and see what it has to offer. You can see right out the gate that there are quite a few programs built in that aim to help you learn to do various things, which betray the origin of Raspberry Pi as something intended to help underprivileged people learn about computer science and programming in general.

So now, you're confronted with your operating system. If you've never used a Linux operating system before, you more than likely have a few questions. Moreover, even if you have used a Linux operating system before, there's the chance that this is not anything like what you've used before if you've primarily stuck to KDE distributions. So let's answer some questions first.

What am I looking at? The answer to that question is simple: Raspbian. Raspbian is a distribution of the Linux operating system, which you've most likely heard of before. It's an offshoot of a popular Linux distribution called Debian. There are many other Linux distributions, one of which is Ubuntu. Raspbian has been designed to be a perfect match for the Raspberry Pi's hardware demands and its specific CPU architecture.

What is Linux?

Linux itself is an offshoot of another operating system from long, long ago called Unix. Unix was extraordinarily famous for various reasons that a book could be written about all on its own (and numerous have, and they are quite good).

Unix itself would inspire many operating systems that people use every day, including Linux (which in itself inspired the extremely popular Android mobile operating system) and macOS (from which the iOS mobile operating system was derived). In other words, if you have a phone or a non-Windows computer, you've already been using a computer inspired by Unix.

Because of its ubiquity in the '80s and the fact that operating systems such as Linux, Minix, and FreeBSD would fit extremely well into the hacker subculture's belief in freedom of information and free software (free as in speech and free as in beer, both), Unix would remain the king of the software development world for quite a long time. Quite a long time leads up to the current day, where you're sitting in front of an unfamiliar operating system wondering what to do.

How quaint

Let's look for a second at our operating system. First, the most important part of a Linux system is the Terminal. If you use an Apple computer, you've probably poked around in the Terminal a few times as well. The Terminal was one of the most heavily used features of Unix because it offered an extremely easy way to get packages, manage your system, and do much, much more. This remains true today. Understanding Linux systems means, to an extent, understanding how the Terminal works and all of the many different things that you can do with it. So, if you want to have an idea of how Linux works, poke your head around a guide aimed at teaching you how the Terminal works.

One of the prime pulls of Linux, too, is the fact that it's completely free, and this applies here no less. You can poke around your system's information and have complete control over the computer and its motherboard. This is why so many geeks like me love Raspbian: it's easy to use, but it offers all of the control and autonomy that Linux distributions do.

You'll notice that Raspbian comes with quite a few different things packed in. Of note is a program geared at helping you with algebra related problems called Mathematica. You'll also notice that there is a version of Chromium included. This browser is much like Google Chrome. It is just the open-source version of Google Chrome. There's a difference between standard versions of Chromium and this version, though; this version is much lighter weight than other versions, and as a result, it runs much better on the Raspberry Pi's delicate architecture. You can open as many tabs as you want! (Don't open as many tabs as you want, it won't go well.)

The last thing of note is the fact that the operating system comes with a version of Minecraft, which is referred to as Minecraft Pi. This is a lot like Minecraft, except it's geared towards helping kids learn how to program. However, you might find it kind of fun if you poke around and try it. Besides, this is a long book, so it won't hurt to give yourself a bit of a break to play a game.

Linux is the best choice for tinkerers. There are many reasons. The first is that it keeps the overall cost of tinkering down since Linux's culture endorses the use of open-source and free software. This means that you can spend a lot less money obtaining software and a lot more time using your software. The fact that it's completely open is great as well because if you get to be good enough at programming, you can crack open the source code and modify it as you wish. There are no secrets, and you know exactly what you're getting into. Also, perhaps the biggest pull is the fact that there are so many open-source tools available to you as a Linux programmer. People have been working with Unix-based systems for almost 50 years now, not to mention that the free and open-source software movement has been around for more than 40. Believe me, if there is anything you want to do, there is almost certainly a program out there already that's been written to do exactly that. If there isn't, Linux makes it extremely easy for you to make it yourself.

Embedded Linux

Technically speaking, there is no such thing as Embedded Linux. When we talk of embedded Linux, we use it as an umbrella term to refer to an *embedded system that runs Linux*. An embedded system refers to a piece of computing hardware designed for a singular, specific application. In contrast, a Personal Computer has a multitude of purposes—browsing the Internet, playing video games, or writing eBooks about the Raspberry Pi. Lately, though, the line that separates general-purpose computing devices and embedded systems are blurring. The Raspberry Pi, this book's main topic, can be classified as both. It just depends on the purpose you bestow upon it.

To be clear, embedded systems are still different from general-purpose computers.

They have distinct qualities that are theirs alone. These include the following:

• Their purpose is very specific, and they are often dedicated to this purpose.

• They are usually underpowered. They tend to lack the beefy power that personal computers usually have.

• They operate in a larger system, acting as a hub for other sensors and devices. This is in contrast with PC's, which usually act alone.

• Their roles are often quite significant, thus why they are assigned that specific task.

• They process things in real-time.

You can have an embedded Linux setup by going nuts on the Terminal in Raspbian. The setup is a complicated process, and it assumes you already know a thing or two about technical stuff. Feel free to research it yourself. We still have more things to learn about Pi.

Chapter 3

How to use Raspberry PI

You can run several types of software on the Raspberry Pi, especially in very operating systems – with which you can run your computer. Of all the available operating systems, the most popular one out of these is Raspbian, which is the Raspberry Pi Foundation's official operating system. Raspbian is based on Debian Linux and is made specifically for the Raspberry Pi that features an array of pre-installed add-ons that will help you get started.

Welcome Wizard

When you run Raspbian for the first time, you'll be introduced to the Welcome Wizard. This tool will enable you to configure the settings in Raspbian so that Raspberry Pi will behave just like or close to how you wanted to.

Note: if you want to close the Welcome Wizard, you only need to click the Cancel button at the bottom of the wizard. However. We would advise against this as there are certain features, including the wireless network that won't be able to work until the first set of questions that you get are answered.

After clicking the Next button, there will be a dropdown box for language, country, and time zone, which you need to click per your geographical location. There will also be a checkbox that will allow you to choose the appropriate keyboard layout; if, for instance, you're using a keyboard with a US-layout, then be sure to check the box that says US-layout. If English isn't your first language, but you prefer anyway over your country's native tongue, then click the 'Use English language' checkbox. Then click Next when you're done.

The next screen is about changing the password from the default one which is 'raspberry'– this is strictly for security reasons, and it's a good idea to create a new password just so hackers and bots aren't able to guess easily and have access to your account and so on. Enter your new password in the spaces provided. If you're using a complex password and wish to know what it looks like, then click the take right next to 'Hide characters' to show the password and write it down on a piece of stationary or additional notepad that only you have access to. Remember, you have to reenter the password to be on the safe side. You've done all that, you can click Next.

The next screen will have you set up your Wi-Fi network. You can choose from a range of networks that are already listed with your keyboard or mouse. Choose your desired network's name by clicking on it, before clicking Next. To ensure that your wireless network is secured, you'll need to insert its pre-shared key, which is also its password; this is usually written at the bottom of the router itself or written on a card along with the router. When you click Next, you'll be able to connect to the network. If you prefer not to choose a wireless network, you can click Skip.

Note: Only the Raspberry Pi 3, Pi 4, and Pi Zero W series have built-in wireless networking. If you are using any other model besides the ones mentioned above and one wireless networking capabilities, you'll need to invest in a USB Wi-Fi adapter.

In the next screen, you will have to install some updates for the Raspbian operating system as well as any other software on your Raspberry Pi board. Be advised that the Raspbian should be regularly updated to add new features, improve performance, but, more importantly, fix technical issues. You can click Next to install the updates or click Skip if you want to move on and install them later. Be advised that downloading and installing the updates could take several minutes, so please be patient. After the updates have been installed, a dialog box that says 'System is up-to-date' will appear, after which you only need to click the OK button.

Finally, the last screen of the Welcome Wizard is a simple process known commonly as rebooting, which is when you have to restart your Raspberry Pi so that certain changes can take effect. All you have to do is click on the Reboot button, and your Raspberry Pi system will restart, and this time, the Welcome Wizard will not appear. With that being said, time for action.

Using the Desktop

The Raspbian operating system that is installed in many Raspberry Pi models these days is commonly known as 'Raspbian with the Raspberry Pi Desktop,' which is the system's main graphical user interface. The desktop will be accompanied by a wallpaper in the background with some of the base programs – that you will be using – appearing on top of that wallpaper. You will find a taskbar at the top of your desktop that enables you to load any program you wish to open; tasks in the taskbar represent those programs.

The right side of the menu bar is where you will find the *system tray*. If there are any removable storage devices connected to the Raspberry Pi, like USB memory sticks, then you need to click on the eject symbol to eject and remove them safely. To the far right, you'll find the timer where you can bring up a digital calendar when you click on it.

Next to the timer is the speaker icon; click on the icon using the left mouse button to adjust the audio volume of your system, or you can click the right mouse button so that you can choose the output you want your system to use. Right next to that is the network icon; you'll know that you're connected to a wireless network when you see your network signal strength is displayed in a series of bars, but if you're connected to a wired network, only two arrows will be displayed. You can bring up a list of nearby networks by clicking on the network icon, whereas the Bluetooth icon right next to it will enable you to connect to any Bluetooth device nearby.

To the left of the menu bar, you will find the launcher, where all the programs installed on the Raspbian operating system can be run. Some of the programs will appear as shortcut icons, whereas others that are hidden away somewhere in the menu can be brought up by clicking the raspberry icon located to the far-right side.

Every program in the menu is split into categories and are explicitly named based on their purpose: for example, the Programming category has software that allows us to write programs – we will elaborate in the later chapters – or as the Games category enables you to play whatever games are listed. Please note that we haven't covered every program in this guide, so you're more than welcome to inspect them at your own volition.

Chromium

The first thing to do when you start using your Raspberry Pi board is to open the Chromium web browser: on the top left side of the menu, you need to click the raspberry icon. Move your mouse's cursor to the Internet category and then click the Chromium Web Browser to open it up.

Chromium is not hard to get used to, and those who have used Google's Chrome browser on other computers will find that it is quite similar in operation. Like any other web browser, chromium allows you to open and view websites, communicate with several people around the world using social media platforms, chat sites, and forms, as well as play games and watch videos.

For a better experience, we suggest maximizing the window of your chromium web browser: on the top right side of the chromium window title bar, you'll find three icons. You will need to click the middle, up-arrow icon, which will maximize the window to fill the entire screen. The button to the left of the *maximize* is *minimize* on the taskbar, which will hide the window when you click on it. And to the right of maximizing is the *close* function which, of course, closes the window.

Note: You must save your work before closing the window. Although most programs will give you the warning to save your work when you hit the close button, other programs don't have this facility.

The big white bar with a magnifying glass that sits at the top left-hand side of the Chromium window is the address bar. Click in the address bar, type www.raspberrypi.org, and then hit *ENTER* on your keyboard. The official Raspberry Pi website will open up. You can also perform other searches in the address bar by simply typing 'Raspbian,' 'Educational Computing,' or 'Raspberry Pi.'

When you load Chromium for the first time, several tabs will be shown at the top of the window. You wish to view another tab, click on it, and if you want to close a tab without necessarily closing the browser itself, then click the cross that you will find at a tab's right-hand edge. To open up a new tab, you can click the tab button that is to the extreme right side of one tab, or you can also hold the *CTRL* key down on your keyboard and then press the *T* key before you let go of *CTRL*.

If you want to close the browser, all you have to do is hit the close button at the top-right corner of the window.

File Manager

Any file that you save be it the programs that you write, videos you create, or the images that you download from online – will go right to your *home directory*. To view your home directory, click the raspberry icon once more to pull up the menu, point the mouse over to Accessories, and then click File Manager to load it.

With the file manager, you can browse a variety of folders (also called *directories*) and files that are already there in the Raspberry Pi's microSD card or on any removable storage device such as a USB flash drive that you can connect to the board's USB ports. When you open it for the first time, your home directly opens up automatically. Here, you'll find lines of folders, also called *subdirectories*, which – similar to the menu – are organized in categories. The main subdirectories that you will find include:

Documents: this is where most of the files that you create will be saved up, from poems to short stories and recipes, and more.

Desktop: When you first load Raspbian, this will be the folder that you will see; if you create and save the file in this folder, it will appear on your desktop, which makes it easy to find as well as load.

MagPi: this folder contains the electronic copy of the Raspberry Pi Foundation's official magazine, The MagPi.

Downloads: downloading any file online using the Chromium web browser will be saved in the Downloads folder automatically.

Pictures: This folder is maintained explicitly for pictures, which are technically known as *image files*.

Music: any piece of music you put or create on the Raspberry Pi board will be stored in this folder.

Videos: This folder is reserved for any video that you upload from an external storage device or download from the Chromium web browser.

Public: any file or folder that you store in this folder will be available to other Raspberry Pi users, despite having their own account.

You will notice that the File Manager window is divided into two panes: the left pane displays your Raspberry Pi's directories, whereas the right pane displays the files and subdirectories of the directory chosen in the left pane. If you insert a removable storage device into the USB port of the board, a dialog box will open up, asking you if you'd like to open it in the File Manager; by clicking the OK button, you'll be able to view the files and subdirectories in that device.

You can easily copy your files on a removable device on your Raspberry Pi's microSD card, or even transfer them from the microSD card to your removable device. When you've opened both the removable device and your home directory in separate File

Manager windows, choose the file that you want to move from one window by clicking and holding the left mouse button and then sliding it to the other window before letting go of the mouse button. This process is called *dragging and dropping*.

Another method would be to click once on the file, select the Edit menu, select Copy, click the other window, choose the Edit menu, and then click Paste.

The Move option, which you can find from the Edit menu, is similar in execution, only that it deletes the file from its original home after being copied. A faster way would be to use keyboard shortcuts *CTRL+C* for copying or *CTRL+X* for cutting and pasting via *CTRL+V*.

Note: to copy text, a file, or folder using keyboard shortcuts such as *CTRL+C*; you need first to hold down the key *CTRL*, and present along with the second key C before letting both of them go.

After you're done with that, click the close button on the top left corner of the window to close the File Manager. If there are other windows open, you need to close all of them. If there's a removable device connected to your Raspberry Pi board, you'll have to eject it by clicking the eject button at the top right corner of the screen before you unplug it.

Note: be sure to click the eject button before you unplug your external storage device. If you don't do this, the files in your storage device may become either corrupt or unusable.

LibreOffice Productivity Suite

If you want to write a document, an article, a poem, or anything else written, then the LibreOffice Writer is what you need. If you've used Microsoft Office or Google Docs, then you have a good idea of how to use LibreOffice's word processor.

One thing to note is that LibreOffice might not be installed on every Raspbian OS image by default. And if that's the case, then you can use the Recommended Software tool to install them.

Besides being able to write documents, this word processor also allows you to format them in a variety of creative ways: you can change the font color, size, insert images, tables, charts, add effects, and any other type of content you choose. Like other word processor programs, the LibreOffice Writer will inspect whatever you've written for mistakes, as well as highlight spelling and grammatical errors in red and green, respectively, as you type.

If you don't know what to write, then we suggest writing a passage on everything that you've learned about the Raspberry Pi board and the software installed in it so far. There are several icons at the top of the window that you can experiment with to see what they do: see if you can increase the font size, as well as change the color. If you're uncertain how to get this done, move your mouse cursor over each icon one at a time to see a 'tooltip' that lets you know what the icon is about and what it does. If you're satisfied with what you've written, click the File menu and then choose the Save option to save all of your work. Give your file and name, and then finally click the Save button.

Note: you should always have the decency of saving your work as you'll never know when you might encounter a power outage, short circuit, or any other mishap that would disrupt your work with the Raspberry Pi board.

The LibreOffice Writer is one of many programs that you will find in the LibreOffice productivity suite. Other Office programs included in this suite are:

• LibreOffice Calc: a spreadsheet used for creating charts and graphs and handling numbers.

• LibreOffice Base: a database used for storing, looking up quickly, and analyzing information.

• LibreOffice Impress: a tool used for creating presentation slides as well as running slideshows.

• LibreOffice Draw: an illustration program where you can create diagrams and pictures.

• LibreOffice Math: a tool for creating appropriately formatted mathematical formulae that can also be used in other documents.

LibreOffice is also made available for other computers as well as operating systems. You prefer using it on your Pi system; then you can visit libreoffice.org download the file and then install it on any operating system, be it Linux, Apple Mac OS, or Microsoft Windows.

If you wish to know more about how you can use LibreOffice, click the Help menu. And if you have no more use for it, then you can close LibreOffice Writer by pointing and clicking the close button that is on the top right corner of the window.

Note: many programs have a help menu with which you can learn about a certain program and how you can use it. This can be handy if you are having trouble operating a program.

Recommended Software Tool

Although you already have access to a wide collection of preinstalled software with your Raspbian operating system, you can get more if you like. This is where the Recommended Software tool comes into play as it has some of the best lines of software that you can find.

Be advised that the Recommended Software tool requires an Internet connection for you to operate. Once you're connected, click the raspberry menu icon, move the cursor to Preferences, and then click on Recommended Software. This will open up the tool and start downloading information about any software that's available. Then a list of some of the compatible software packages will appear after a couple of seconds. Like the raspberry menu software, the ones here are also organized in several categories. Click on any category in the left pane to view software under that category, or you can click All Programs to view everything.

If you see any software with a tick right next to it, it means it's already installed on your operating system. And if there's no tick in the box, then use the left mouse button to click the checkbox so you can prepare it for installation. Mark, as many numbers of software you want to prepare for installation. But make sure that there's enough space in your microSD card for these programs; otherwise, you'll have to limit the installation.

Similarly, you can also uninstall software this way: you look for any software with a tick in its checkbox and then left mouse click on the box to remove the tick. But if you have changed your mind or have made a mistake, then you can go back in the previous section and put the tick back in the box again.

When you're all set, click the OK button to start installing or uninstalling the software that you have selected/unselected. After you've downloaded and installed or uninstalled any software in your selection, a message box appears; click the OK button to exit the Recommended Software tool.

The Add/Remove Software tool is another tool that can help you install or uninstall software. It is located in the same Preferences category in the Raspbian menu. There is a wide range of software that is available with this. However, none of them have been approved by the Raspberry Pi Foundation.

Raspberry Pi Configuration Tool

You'll find that it functions similar to the Welcome Wizard that you used in the beginning: you'll be able to change plenty of settings in the Raspbian operating system. First, click the raspberry icon and then move your mouse cursor to the Preferences category, and then select Raspberry Pi Configuration to be loaded.

This tool is divided into four tabs, each controlling a certain part of Raspbian. The first thing you will see when the tool is loaded for the first time is System: you can set up a hostname – this is the name that the Raspberry Pi board uses on your wired or wireless network – change your account password, as well as a bunch of other settings though most of these settings don't require any changing.

Note: this overview is to help you get acquainted with the tool and how to use it.

Move your mouse cursor to the Interfaces tab and click it with your left mouse button to pull up the next category. You'll see a big list of settings that have been disabled. You can only change the settings if you include new software into your Raspberry Pi, including the Raspberry Pi Camera Module, and only if the manufacturer of the hardware instructs you to. The only exceptions here include VNC, which enables a 'Virtual Network Computer' and allows you to see as well as control the Raspbian desktop from another computer on your network thanks to a VNC client; Remote GPIO, where you can use the Raspberry Pi's GPIO pins from another computer on your network; and SSH, where you enable a 'Secure Shell' and enables you to log into the Raspberry Pi using another computer on your network with an SSH client.

When you click on the Performance tab, the third category can be viewed. From here, you can configure the amount of memory that the Raspberry Pi's graphics processing unit (GPU) uses and, depending on some models, increase the performance of your board thanks to a process called *overclocking*. Though, it would be better to leave these settings as they are unless you need to change them.

Lastly, you get to view the final category by clicking the Localization tab. From here, you can set up your locale, in which you can control how the numbers are displayed, the language used in Raspbian, change the layout of your keyboard, change the time zone, and also set up your country for Wi-Fi capabilities. As of now, however, you need to exit the tool by clicking the Cancel button without making any further changes.

Warning: there are different rules for different countries about the kind of frequencies that are Wi-Fi radio can use. For instance, if you set the Wi-Fi country in the Raspberry Pi Configuration Tool to a country other than the one that you're in right now, it will confuse your device and have a struggle when connecting to your networks. What's worse, is that it can also be illegal under radio licensing laws. So, in other words, don't do it.

Shutting Down

After exploring the Raspbian desktop and having your way with it, it's time to learn how to shut your Raspberry Pi down safely. Like any other computer that people use, the Raspberry Pi stores your files in *volatile memory* – which is a memory that gets emptied as soon as the system is powered off. For every document you make, it's important to save as you type – this is where your files will be transferred to a *non-volatile memory*, which is the microSD card – so that you can retrieve the files that you saved and resume working on them.

But the documents that you're working on aren't the only ones opened. The operating system Raspbian several files opened while running, and if for any reason, the power cable is pulled from the Raspberry Pi board as the files are still opened, it could lead to the entire operating system becoming corrupt. You'll have to install it all over again.

So, to prevent this from occurring, you need to instruct Raspbian to save all of your files and documents and prepare itself for when it's time to be powered off – a process known as *shutting down.*

Warning: remember not to pull the power cable out of the Raspberry Pi board until you shut it down first. If you don't do this, it will corrupt Raspbian, and you could end up losing any file that you created or downloaded.

To shut down, click the raspberry icon at the top left corner of the desktop and then select Shutdown. A dialog box with three options will show up: Shut down, Logout, and Reboot. Shut down is the option that you mostly use clicking this will instruct the operating system to shut all open files and software, shutting the entire system down. When you see the display turn black, with a couple of seconds until the green flashing light on the Pi disappears, that's when it's safe to turn the power supply off.

And if you want to turn the Raspberry Pi back on, all you have to do is disconnect and then reconnect the power cable, or you can toggle the power switch at the wall socket.

The remote process is similar to Shutdown, it will close every one of your files, but instead of shutting down, it will restart your Raspberry Pi – similar to if you had chosen the shutdown option, and then had to disconnect and reconnect the power cable. Certain changes you make with your Raspberry Pi require a restart to implement them – like installing certain core software updates – or if the software has crashed and has left your operating system in an unusable state.

And lastly, the Logout feature, which is quite useful if there is more than one account on your Raspberry Pi: it will close any program that you currently have running and will immediately bring up the login screen for which you can access another account using their designated username and password. And if by mistake you hit Logout, then you can get back in by simply typing 'pi' as your username and the password you chose in the Welcome Wizard.

Data and Variables

The first thing that we're going to look at is mathematical program operations and how you can perform them. To understand this, though, you need to understand a thing or two about data.

Python understands data in a relatively unique way, but there's a reason that it's relative; all programming languages understand data in this same kind of detached manner. Data is, for lack of a better term, any singular piece of information that is used to represent some given concept. Any individual piece of data is referred to as a value. **Values** can take on several different forms.

However, under it all, computers don't actually understand any of these different forms; instead, computers understand the raw idea of ones and zeroes, binary calculations that are happening far, far under the hood of the computer. On top of the binary code is one layer of abstraction, known as Assembly code, which operates upon the bits, or the different sets of binary code that represent individual values. On top of that is another layer of abstraction, known as the operating system. Then there's yet another layer of abstraction, the programming language in use. This works with the operating system to convert something that we can understand into assembly language, which the computer's processor then converts into a set of different calculations. All of this happens in the matter of micro or even nanoseconds.

The key point of all of this is that computers understand things in terms of ones and zeroes, and the way that we see a value means next to nothing to a computer. In order to solve this, programmers long ago decided that computers would categorize different values into different *types*. These types of data tell the computer how and in what manner to perform operations to the given values as they correspond to the ones and zeroes. This is a super complex architecture, so don't feel too bad if it doesn't immediately make a whole lot of sense.

Anyhow, in pursuit of properly understanding all of this, we must start to break down these data types a little bit and look at them with a more abstract eye than we currently are. So let's do that. The next thing that we're going to do is take a sincere look at the different kinds of data that you can use in Python.

Integer

The integer data type refers to any piece of data that corresponds to a whole number in our abstract understanding. Therefore, these would be numbers such as 7, 39, or -3.

Float

The float data type refers to any piece of data that corresponds to a decimal number in our abstract understanding, so things such as 3.141569 or 94.3332.

Double

Double stands for "double precision" number and refers to a very specific kind of decimal number. You don't need to understand this *too* in-depth at this point because of float and double act rather synonymously in Python. The reason for this distinction goes back to a time when computers had less RAM and less processing power than they do now, but for our purposes, you can largely ignore this.

Boolean

Boolean means true or false. This will make a lot more sense later on when we start to talk about programmatic logic and the way that logic actually plays a part in computer science.

Character

The character stands for any singular alphanumeric or symbolic character that can be printed out in a computer console. These could be things like A, 3, or $. This is a fickle understanding, though, because characters correlate to an ASCII value, which means that any given character also has a numeric integer value. For this reason, if you had the character "3" and the integer 3 and tried to see if they were the same, they wouldn't be. Bear this in mind as you program.

String

We'll talk about strings more in-depth later, but strings are essentially long chains of characters that are put together. Any set of character values is a string, whether it is 2 characters or 2000 characters long.

These are not all of the values available for you to use in Python. However, they are the ones that you are most likely to use almost immediately, so we've covered them here for that reason specifically. These values may be expressed in any given expression in Python. For example:

```
print(3 + 3)
```

would print 6

```
print("Hey there!\n")
```

printing a string to the console

```
print('C')
```

printing a character to the console

In other words, these form the very nucleus of everything that you're going to be doing in programming. Every piece of code you ever write will be working with values like these and manipulating them in one way or another. As you work with more and more code, you'll come to appreciate how truly often you make use of all of this and how every statement in a program is just the manipulation of data in one way or another. This is the nature of programming, for better or worse.

Sometimes, you're going to want to keep up with these data pieces so that you can recall them or change them at a later point. What can you do for this purpose? The answer is simple. You can use **variables**. Variables offer a method by which you can keep track of values over a long period as you work through a program.

Recall earlier how we talked about data types. Data types were especially useful and a bit more diverse than they are in Python because Python tries to go out of its way to make things easy for you; however, all of these values are stored in the computer's memory, and they're stored in boxes of pre-allocated size depending on how much space any given data type uses.

These individual boxes in the computer's memory can be referred to as variables. Picture it like the overhead view of a given city. You may have a bunch of lots that you can place houses in. You then will refer to any given lot by its address. The lot is like the variable itself, and the address is the **name** of the variable.

Therefore, you can actually store all of these values in variables where you decide the name to refer to it by. So, let's say that you had a variable called something like **dogAge**. If your dog was 4 years old, then you may set this like so:

dogAge = 4

If your dog's name was Lucky, then you may set a string variable like so:

dogName = "Lucky"

Python makes it extremely easy to name and declare variables.

Some other languages have a bunch more hurdles to the process, but Python most definitely does not. This can be both a blessing and a curse. In other languages, you may have to say the type of the variable when you declare it, but Python takes this burden off you. Why would this be a bad thing? Well, simply put, it can be confusing for a newer programmer who doesn't have much experience working with different data types. You may end up forgetting and trying to make a comparison between two pieces of data that aren't of the same time, actually messing up your data in the meantime because the computer doesn't compare different pieces of data in the same way.

This is the reason that you actually want to learn what the individual data types are. It will help you realize, for example, that the string "34" and the integer 34 are not the same and should not be compared, and may explain to you why your comparisons may be off at one point or another if you're not careful about this.

Python Math

Of course, working with variables is much more useful if you're actually doing operations on the data in question—for example, if you're actively performing math operations or performing useful equations. In this section, we're going to be exploring the different ways in which you can work with data.

Bear in mind primarily that you can refer back to variables. For example, if you wanted to print a string that you saved in a variable, you could do it like so:

print(dogName)

Or, if you were ambitious and wanted to print out your dog's name and dog's age both, you could do it like so:

print("My dog's name is " + dogName + " and they are " + dogAge + " years old.")

But what if something changed? What if, for example, your dog aged by a year? What could you do?

Well, you'd want to take your dog's age and then add one to it. But how can you do this? Well, you can do this by actually assigning it a new value. You can reassign values to variables and manipulate the variables that they have much like you set them and initialized them in the first place. The process is similar for the most part. Let's say, for example, that we wanted to add 1 to the variable dogAge. We could do that like so:

dogAge = dogAge + 1

The variable dogAge would take the old value of dogAge, 4, ,and add 1 to it, and this would be set as the new value for the variable **dogAge**. Make sense? Therefore, if you printed the variable dogAge now, it would print out the number 5:

print(dogAge)

Python has numerous different operators that you can use to do the math. The Python mathematical operators are like so:

c + d

This is the addition operator. It is used to add one number to another.

c - d

This is the subtraction operator. It is used to subtract one number from another.

c * d

This is the multiplication operator. It is used to multiply one number by another.

c / d

This is the division operator. It is used to divide one number by another.

c % d

This is the modulo operator. It is used to find the remainder when you divide c by d. For example, 7 % 3 would yield 1 since 7 divided by 3 has a remainder of 1.

These are the primary different mathematical operators in Python that you need to know. Using this knowledge, you can carry out complex mathematical operations in Python and make some really cool things happen. But this is only the beginning!

Let's note for a second that the way that we reassigned a value earlier wasn't necessarily the best way to do it. That is to say that the statement "dogAge = dogAge + 1" can easily be shortened and made easier to both read and understand. There are a few different shorthand operators in Python for assignment. These are as such:

c += d

This just means c = c + d.

```
c -= d
```

This just means c = c - d.

```
c *= d
```

This means c = c * d.

```
c /= d
```

This means c = c / d.

```
c %= d
```

This means c = c % d.

As you can see, these operators aren't terribly difficult to understand, but they can go a long way to simplify your code and making it easier to read as a whole.

Comments

Comments are essential for programming unless you want to get lost in your own code. It is especially important when working with a team. Comments are parts of code that, from the computer's perspective, do **absolutely nothing**. Why is it important, then? Comments are important so that you can insert text in your code and not have it affect the program itself. You can use these to tell your fellow programmer not to touch a certain part of the code because it's currently a band-aid solution as you try to fix another part of the code. For our purposes, you can use this as a guide for yourself so you know what part of the code does what and how.

Formatting

If you've ever programmed in another language, then you'll have noticed by now that Python is quite different in many ways. Not the least of these ways is how Python handles formatting. Many popular languages are ambivalent in regards to whitespace; a semicolon separates statements, and you could put your whole program on the same line if you really wanted to. There are even competitions in languages like C and Java to obfuscate code and make it as pretty as possible at the expense of readability.

Python, on the other hand, cares a *lot* about whitespace. Whitespace in Python—that is, line breaks, spaces, and tabs—indicates to Python the hierarchy of the code. This is the main engine by which Python actually starts to understand your code, so you need to pay close attention to your whitespace. Make sure that you're indenting things just as I do and paying attention to how the indentations actually affect the flow of your code as well as how your code works altogether.

User Input and Casting

Here, we're going to spend a brief minute talking about taking in user input. There are going to be many times where you're going to need to retrieve information from the user. For example, you may be asking for the name of the file or some kind of data necessary to the program from the user. It may even be something as innocuous as a book title if you're writing something like a library or bookkeeping program. One way or another, programs thrive not off just existing but off interaction and their ability to interact with the user and make things happen.

Because of this, you must understand how user input in Python works. It's relatively simple.

All user input in Python—at least using the console—is handled through the ***input*** method. The input method allows you to take in information from the console. It will read everything up until the Enter button is pressed and return all of that information as a string.

The input method works like so:

input("Prompt text")

You can set the prompt text to whatever you want or leave it out entirely. All prompt text indicates is that the text that is fed to the input method, as an argument, will be displayed to the user in question.

You can set the input method as the value of a variable, and this will set whatever the user enters as the value of that variable. For example, if my text were like so:

food = input("What is the last thing you ate?")

and the user entered ***nachos***, then the value of ***food*** would be ***nachos***. Therefore, if we printed the variable ***food***, it would print as nachos:

print(food)

 # would print as nachos

Sometimes, though, this isn't the end of the line. Let's say that you were writing a calculator program, and you needed to accept numbers that the user entered. Of course, the input method returns a ***string***. You know from our discussions earlier about how data types work that strings are not the data type that we need at the moment; no, we need a float value or an integer value. So how can we convert whatever the user entered into one of those values?

You can do this by casting. **Casting** is simply the conversion of one data type to another data type. In Python, variables can hold any data type, so you can actually just set the casted data type as the new value for the old variable, but you don't really want to do this just for the sake of maintaining clean code and being, well, a good programmer. In fact, it's probably best that you avoid this particular plan at all costs and just make new variables because it's more readable and secure anyway. Use a single variable for your user input and then just set your other variables as the casted form of that. For example:

in = input("What is the number?")

number = #casted in

Casting values is easy. All that you do is put the type you're trying to cast them to in between parentheses right next to the value, like so:
number = (float)in

This would set the value of the **number** to be the value of **in** casted to a float. Python automatically handles these tricky type conversions for you, for the most part, so you don't have a whole lot to worry about there.

Chapter 4

Interfacing Hardware

Interfacing to the Raspberry PI Inputs/Outputs

In this chapter, you will learn about GPIOs and interfacing. It's crucial to learn about this subject because understanding the fundamental concepts can facilitate the formation of custom electronics circuits that are controlled and interfaced from within an embedded Linux.

The GPIO

Raspberry Pi features an expansion header with forty pins. These pins are numbered from 1 to 40.

[Source: http://geek-university.com/raspberry-pi/ raspberry-pi-board/]

These GPIO pins are as follows:

Raspberry Pi B+ J8 Header

Pin#	NAME			NAME	Pin#
01	3.3v DC Power	⊙ ⊙		DC Power 5v	02
03	GPIO 2 (SDA1, I2C)	⊙ ⊙		DC Power 5v	04
05	GPIO 3 (SCL1, I2C)	⊙ ●		Ground	06
07	GPIO 4 (GPIO_GCLK)	⊙ ⊙		(TXD0) GPIO14	08
09	Ground	● ⊙		(RXD0) GPIO15	10
11	GPIO17 (GPIO_GEN0)	⊙ ⊙		(GPIO_GEN1) GPIO18	12
13	GPIO27 (GPIO_GEN2)	⊙ ●		Ground	14
15	GPIO22 (GPIO_GEN3)	⊙ ⊙		(GPIO_GEN4) GPIO23	16
17	3.3v DC Power	⊙ ⊙		(GPIO_GEN5) GPIO24	18
19	GPIO10 (SPI_MOSI)	⊙ ●		Ground	20
21	GPIO9 (SPI_MISO)	⊙ ⊙		(GPIO_GEN6) GPIO25	22
23	GPIO11 (SPI_CLK)	⊙ ⊙		(SPI_CE0_N) GPIO 8	24
25	Ground	● ⊙		(SPI_CE1_N) GPIO 7	26
27	ID_SD (I2C ID EEPROM)	⊙ ⊙		(I2C ID EEPROM) ID_SC	28
29	GPIO 5	⊙ ●		Ground	30
31	GPIO 6	⊙ ⊙		GPIO12	32
33	GPIO13	⊙ ●		Ground	34
35	GPIO19	⊙ ⊙		GPIO16	36
37	GPIO26	⊙ ⊙		GPIO20	38
39	Ground	● ⊙		GPIO21	40

Rev 1.1
16/07/2014
http://www.element14.com

The expansion header contains different types of pins.

The light red pin is connected to the 5V rail of the Raspberry Pi. It's consistent at +5 V.

The dark red pin is connected to the 3.3V rail of the Raspberry Pi. It's consistent at +3.3 V.

The black pin is connected to the ground of the Raspberry Pi. It's consistent at 0 V.

The yellow pin is a new addition. It is seen on the Raspberry Pi Model B+. The I2C bus is dedicated to the expansion boards.

The rest of the pins are called General Purpose Input/Output (GPIO). This GPIO is a generic pin on the circuit. Its behavior, regardless of whether it is an output or an input, is controllable by the user at run time.

These GPIO pins are also connected to +3.3V rails. If you use them for input, they can read voltages. If you use them for output, they can be set to 0 V for low and +3.3 V for high.

Different Types of GPIO Pins

The green pins are generic GPIO pins that do not have any special purposes.

The blue pins may be used as I2C bus or GPIO.

The orange pins may be utilized for UART or as GPIO.

The purple pins may be used as SPI bus or as GPIO.

All in all, there are twenty-four GPIO ports. Even though you can use any GPIO pins, you should use the green ones first as much as possible.

Interfacing Electronics

Your Raspberry Pi would be useless if you weren't able to use it to interact and use other electronic devices, wouldn't it? Here, we'll discuss how to set up your Pi to work with other electronics. First, you'll need to have the proper equipment to make sure you won't destroy your circuit or even your Pi.

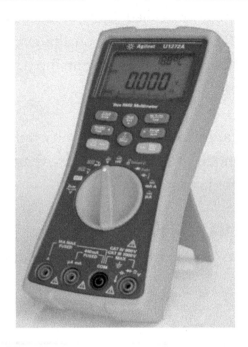

Digital Multimeter

You must have one of these before starting to tinker with circuitry. This device measures many things, such as voltage, current, resistance, etc. This ensures that you don't accidentally pump your circuit with more than it can handle.

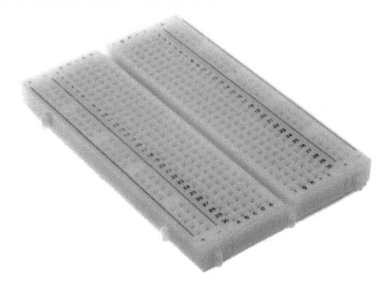

Breadboard

A breadboard is a base for you to use when making prototypes for electronics. Before trying things out on your Raspberry Pi, try it on a breadboard first. Make sure to get the good ones!

Discrete Components

Diodes

A diode is a semiconductor component that simply allows one current to flow in one direction but not the other.

Light Emitting Diodes (LEDs)

An LED acts similarly to a diode, just that it emits light if the current flows in the correct direction. These come in many shapes, sizes, and colors. The length of the leg determines which leg is positive (cathode) and which is negative (anode).

Capacitors

A capacitor is a component that can be used to store electrical energy. It stores energy when there is a difference in voltage between its two plates. Once the voltage difference dissipates, it releases the stored energy.

Transistors

A transistor is a semiconductor component that can be used to amplify or switch electricity or electric signals.

Optocouplers

These are digital switching devices that allow you to isolate two electrical circuits from one another.

Buttons and Switches

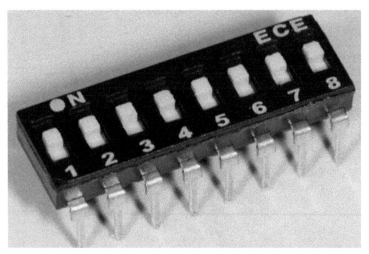

These are quite self-explanatory. These are the input devices that you interact with to make your circuit do something. Their basic function is to open or close a circuit. They come in different shapes and forms, depending on what you need.

Communication Protocols

For embedded systems to work harmoniously, there needs to be communication between them. This is how data is transferred between embedded systems. There are specific standards that are set in place to make sure there is consistency and coherence in their communication. These are communication protocols.

Some communication protocols exist, and the difference between them would be better understood if you learn these few concepts first:

Bit rate

The bit rate describes the number of bits that are sent per unit of time. This is usually described in bits/sec.

Baud rate

Whereas the bit rate describes the number of bits sent per unit of time, the baud rate describes the number of symbols sent per unit of time. These *symbols* can each be of any number of bits. This depends on the design. If ever the symbols are only 1 bit, the baud rate would be equal to the bit rate.

Parallel Communication

In parallel communication, multiple bits are sent at the same time.

Serial Communication

In serial communication, bits are sent one bit at a time.

Synchronous Serial Communication

This describes a serial communication protocol wherein data is sent at a steady, continuous stream at a constant rate. This requires that the internal clocks of the two embedded systems be synchronized at the same rate so that the receiver receives the signal at the same intervals that the transmitter used.

Asynchronous Serial Communication

This form of serial communication does not require synchronized internal clocks. In place of the synchronization signal, the data stream instead contains start and stop signals before and after the transmission, respectively. When the receiver receives the start signal, it prepares for a stream of data. Conversely, when it receives the stop signal, it resets to its previous state to receive a new stream. Now that you've learned about the basic concepts of communication between embedded systems, we can now learn about the different communication protocols.

I2C

I2C is short for Inter-Integrated Circuit. It is asynchronous serial communication protocol that uses two wires: one for data (SDA), and one for the clock (SCL). It is a multi-master, multi-slave serial computer bus. Most of its uses are confined to attaching lower-speed peripheral integrated circuits to processors and microcontrollers. Because of how it works, I2C must validate the data passing through it by evaluating whether or not the data on the SDA line changes when the SCL is high. The data on the SDA line should only ever change when the SCL is low. Otherwise, the data is rendered invalid.

I2C supports a wide range of voltages.
I2C is half-duplex.

I2C can support serial 8-bit data transfers up to a speed of 100kbps. This is the standard clock speed of SCL. I2C is also capable of a higher bitrate: 400 kbps (fast mode) and 3.4 Mbps (high-speed mode).

I2C is mainly used for short-distance communication.

UART

UART is short for Universal Asynchronous Receiver Transmitter. In this protocol, one wire is used for transmitting, and another wire is used for receiving. UART uses a serial type of communication; therefore, bits travel in one wire.

UART supports communication through RS232.

Standard baud rates for UART include 110, 300, 600, 1200, 4800, and 9600.

UART can only support communication between two devices at any one time. This is because it is a point-to-point communication protocol.

SPI

SPI is short for the Serial Peripheral Interface. It is an asynchronous serial communication interface protocol used for short-distance communication. It can operate with one master and several slave devices.

SPI is a full-duplex type of communication protocol.
SPI protocol has no limit for message size, making it very flexible.

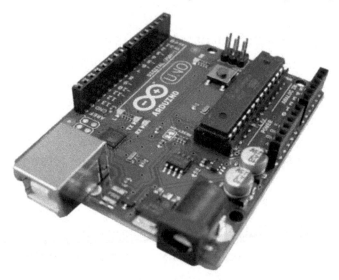

Real-Time Interfacing Using Arduino

In case you aren't familiar, an Arduino is a powerful microcontroller. You can use it in tandem with a Raspberry Pi, creating some impressive projects. Obviously, you'll need an Arduino for this to work. You'll need a lot of programming expertise and mastery of interfaces to make use of this and explaining that will make this book longer than it needs to be, so feel free to do some further research on this topic. However, I'll discuss a few key things.

You can interface with the Arduino using any of the communication protocols discussed above (I2C, UART, and SPI).

You can configure the Arduino as an I2C slave. This means you can connect several Arduinos to one Raspberry Pi.

A straightforward UART connection can only support one slave at a time.

If you require a fast, high-level interaction between your Arduino and Pi, configuring the Arduino as an SPI slave will be the way to go. This is because the Arduino's clock speed will only limit an SPI connection.

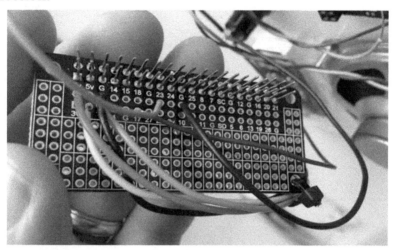

Input and Output

You probably have noticed that row of pins along the top edge of the Raspberry Pi board. These are the GPIO pins. GPIO is short for General Purpose Input/Output. Using the software, you can designate whether each of these pins is for input or output. You can do many things with this.

Two of these pins are 5V, and two more are 3.3V. There are also several ground pins, which you cannot configure. The rest are general-purpose 3V3 pins.

If you designate a pin to be an output pin, you can set it to high, at 3V3, or low, at 0V. Conversely, input pins can be read as high (3V3) or low (0V).

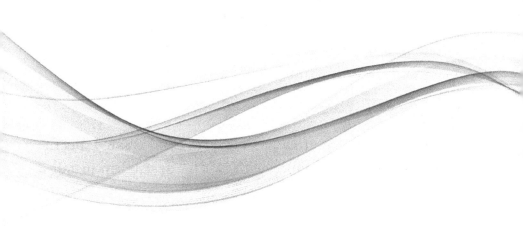

Chapter 5

Download the Operating System

Downloading and Installing Raspberry Pi

You are not going to be able to run Raspberry Pi without first downloading the operating system.

You can find the software you need at www.RaspberryPi.org.

Noobs

Noobs is a great program for Pi beginners. The word noobs stands for new out of the box software. If you want to, you can download a card that has noobs preinstalled on it from any retailer that sells Pi products. Or, you can go to the Raspberry Pi website and download it from there.

Noobs is easy to use an operating system that has Raspbian installed on it for you to choose and download an operating system off the internet for your computer.

Noobs Lite is using the same installer but without downloading Raspbian. Everything is a thing else is going to be the same.

Raspbian

This is the official operating system that was created by the foundation and can be installed with NOOB, or you can install it on its own.

Most Raspbian is going to come with the software you need to be preinstalled so that you can do more educational programming than you would be able to on NOOBS. Raspbian is also going to come with several different programming languages installed with it.

There is a PIXEL image that lies inside of a ZIP file on the Raspbian operating system where all your features are going to be archived, but the old tools that were used to unzip these files are not going to be supported on all platforms.

If your download for Raspbian is corrupted or is not opening correcting, you are going to want to attempt to use 7Zip or The Unarchiever before trying a reinstall.

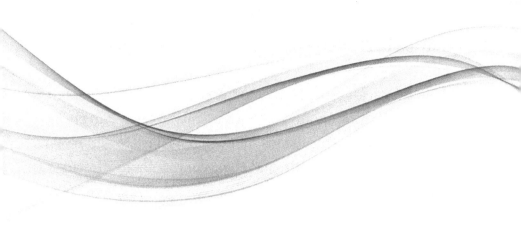

Chapter 6
Projects

LibreELEC Media Center

LibreELEC is a multimedia center in which you can turn just about any TV into a smart TV. You can use it to download apps, access hard disks, and play movie files from the remote PC on the TV.

You can also receive internet radio broadcasts and stream them to your sound system. Additionally, there is a Spotify app for LibreELEC if you have an account. This is a project where Raspberry Pi can make itself useful in everyday life.

Homebridge

An exciting project in the area of Smart-Home is the project Homebridge (homebridge.io). This software-based project is relatively easy to implement. By using Homebridge, even non-Apple certified Smart-Home devices can be used with Apple's

HomeKit and be controlled without any additional apps.

The whole thing can be implemented very easily with a Raspberry Pi. The practical thing about it is that the software is relatively easy to install and control. This means that you only have to add plugins from different manufacturers and then control them directly via Apple's HomeKit.

The picture below shows two virtual lamps that can be switched on and off directly. You can easily add such devices later in HomeKit with a simple QR code. Just scan the code with the photo app, and you can control the device from your iPhone, iPad, or even your Mac.

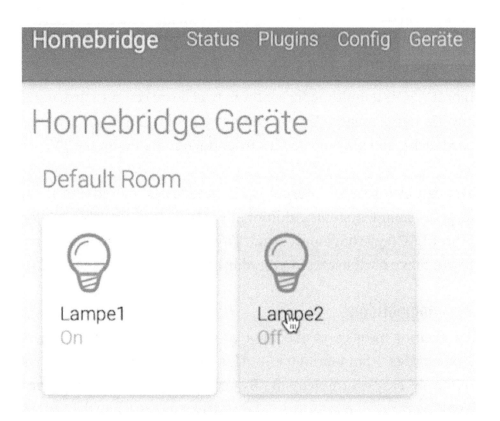

And the whole thing is very easy to install. This will be discussed later in this manual.

MagicMirror

Another interesting project from the area of Smart-Home is the project MagicMirror (magicmirror.builders). The software is relatively easy to install. You can use it to set up a display in the mirror, which you can hang in your house or apartment. In the mirror, you can display various information, such as time and weather. The mirror can also be connected to other Smart-Home devices. So, the project is a very nice gimmick, which can be easily realized with a little tinkering.

Pi-Hole Ad-Blocker

Another useful project we will look at in this book is the Pi-Hole project (pi-hole.net). Pi-Hole is a network-wide advertising blocker that can be installed on the Raspberry Pi.

If you redirect the Internet settings on your router to Pi-Hole, all Internet traffic will be filtered through the Raspberry Pi. From this point on, the pi-hole server will ensure that, for example, most advertisements on each device are filtered out. We will take a closer look at this later in the book to see how it works in detail.

RetroPi Game-Console

This is a special operating system where old arcade and console games up to Playstation 1 can be emulated and played on the Raspberry Pi. This project is a nice opportunity to recreate in your free time or to spend time with your kids.

Chapter 7

Raspberry with Python and Linux

Raspberry pi with Linux Systems

When it comes to embedded systems, startup time is crucial. For example, when you switch on your TV, your goal is to start watching your favorite show within five seconds of pressing the power button. So, how can you develop a program that can boot quickly and not need any other kind of user input to work? Well, you can use embedded systems programming, which is also referred to as bare-metal programming.

If you want to enable the boot loader of the Raspberry Pi and be able to run your desired program, you have to strip the Raspbian operating system of your micro SD card as well as load certain files onto it. This way, you can directly access the hardware and find out how you can turn a couple of LEDs on and off with the use of GPIO pins.

You want your Raspberry Pi to function as an embedded system. After the operating system has been stripped off, you can start programming your desired functionality with the use of an assembly. You will be accessing the hardware as instructed by the manufacturer.

So what are embedded systems exactly? They refer to computers that do not feature any operating systems. They are typically created for specific purposes.

In the past, for instance, all systems used embedded systems for computing because there were no operating systems yet. At present, these embedded systems remain available for specialized applications.

In addition, embedded programming is ideal for firmware due to its time benefits. Just think of your own Mac or PC. How much time does it take to boot up after you hit the power button?

The majority of the startup time is affected by the complexity of the operating system you have on your computer. Moreover, while you use your computer in the operating system environment, it's hardware does a lot of work to run several background processes.

Through embedded systems, you can be freed from performance restraints. They get rid of the operating system and directly run the program from a hard drive. This lets the device boot up within a short period as well as utilize the performance of your hardware well.

This may seem very appealing. You may even wonder why not all programs run this way. Well, convenience is a key factor. The needs of the system should also be considered. This is the reason why a lot of computers did not become famous before Microsoft and Apple came into the market.

The development of a graphically driven interface lets users access computers with relative ease. The operating system, despite killing performance and loading very slowly, was useful and convenient. In fact, a lot of individuals, including the developers themselves, were amazed by its advantages.

Then again, this does not mean that computers were not useful before the invention of the operating system. Embedded systems were actually highly beneficial before the development of the operating system.

In addition, computers that use operating systems are usually multi-purpose devices. A lot of people have to do spreadsheets, word processing, mathematical computations, and internet browsing, among other activities. They need something that can allow them to do all of that with just one machine.

Such variety calls for a more complicated system that makes use of various hardware for various purposes. On the other hand, embedded systems tend to focus on dealing with just one piece of equipment with a narrower functionality scope.

How to Program Embedded Systems

Instead, you have to use something that computers can understand. You need to communicate using a language that would sound native to them.

You need to compile your assembly into your kernel that the Raspberry Pi will look into, rather than the usual Raspbian kernel. For this to happen, you have to strip off all data from the SD card of the Raspberry Pi. You need something to load the kernel into. See to it that you always keep a backup of your data.

Kernels typically act as bridges between the software and the hardware. The Raspbian kernel makes it easier for users to acquire data from their monitor or keyboard and then manipulate it.

However, in embedded systems, there is no need for you to communicate with most of the hardware. There's also no need for a

GUI. You can make your way around without using it.

Embedded design is generally programmed for specific purposes. For example, you may want a couple of LEDs to blink. Hence, you need to have a system that is time-sensitive for booting since you have to take away anything that is not needed to make LEDs blink.

Linux Usage

Commands

- They refer to advanced and basic commands used in Linux

Tex editors

- These refer to a set of text editors used for the Raspberry Pi

Root

- The prefix "sudo" and the user "root"

Users

- Allows for setting up multiple users on the Raspberry Pi system

Scripting

- It refers to the combination of commands to perform complex actions

Crontab/Cron

- It sets up pre-scheduled tasks

.bash and .bashrc aliases

- They are your aliases and shell configuration

rc.local

- It refers to the initialization configuration

Additional Help for Beginners

The following are explanations of some of the basic uses of Linux, as well as the commands used to get around the Raspberry Pi.

The Linux File System

- This is where files are kept, the software is installed, and danger zones are seen, among others. It contains Home, Whole File System, and Backup.

Home

- This is where files are kept. It is the home folder

Whole File System

- It refers to the rest of the file system of Linux

Backup

- It backs up files as well as operating system images

Raspberry Pi and Python

Python language presents a high-level syntax; we say this because its form of writing is very close to human language. Also, Python supports object-orientation.

Fundamentally, python requires precise writing of code. Still, it also offers a friendly user interface where you are guided along the way of writing codes by the application itself (marking mistakes in code and offering useful suggestions).

This specific integrated development environment for python has two modes, a normal mode, and a Simple mode. The simple mode makes things even easier for beginners, and in this guide, we will be referring to the Simple model of this application.

This is the toolbar that you'll see while in the application's Simple

Mode. Beneath each friendly icon on the toolbar, you'll see that they are labeled with the purpose for which they are used.

This is the application's script area. The purpose of this area is precisely similar to the Scratch application. We write down codes in this area, the numbering on the left side of this area indicates the line number. As you keep writing codes, it's automatically indexed. In the scenario where your code encounters an error, you will know which line of code the error is referring to and because every line is indexed, you can quickly navigate to the faulty line of code and fix it. This simple indexing can be useful and timesaving. This is the Python Shell. This area provides information about the code which is currently being run by the application and, you can input individual lines of code and execute them by merely pressing the ENTER button.

This is specifically the variables area. This area shows you information (name and value) of all the variables that you created for a specific program.

Programming with Python: Making a Program

After you start up python, the first thing you will notice is that, unlike Scratch, there are no colorful blocks or sprites. This is because Python is more of a traditional programming language that relies on code being manually written down (without any typos or errors, of course!).

Open up python from the Raspberry Pi menu and wait for Thonny Python IDE to load up (Thonny will startup in the Simple Mode by default). Go over to the Python shell area and type in

Print("Good Morning!")

After typing in the following instruction, all you need to do is press the ENTER key, and you'll see the message "Good Morning" displayed below the instruction. We have just created our first program. It was as simple as that!

As soon as you hit ENTER, the code will execute. On the other hand, when you press ENTER after writing a line of code, instead of executing the lines of code, you just get a new blank line to write more code. To execute the codes in the scripts area, you need to do so by clicking the 'Run' icon in the toolbar (When you click the Run button, Thonny will prompt you to save your current program first, just type in a name for your program and click save). Notice that when you run a saved program from the scripts area, the message in the shell area is a bit different this time

>>> %Run 'Name you used to save the program.py.'

Good Morning!

You can also write the same line of code in the scripts area as well, but this time, we'll use a different and more popular phrase "Hello, World!" and while saving it, we will give it the name Hello, World!

(Here's the message you'll see in the shell area)

>>> %Run 'Hello World.py'

Hello, World!

The First line instructs the Interpreter to execute the program, which has just been saved, and the second line is the result or the output of running that program, in our case, displaying a message. We have successfully written our first program on Python and ran it in both interactive and script modes.

Using Loops and Code Indentation

Indentation is basically python's way of controlling the sequence in which the lines of code are executed. In Scratch programming, we would use the colorful blocks and place them above each other in the sequence, which we wanted, but in Python, we need to use indentation to tell the computer that this is the sequence in which the lines of code are to be run.

Open a new project by clicking on the 'New' icon in the toolbar. This will open a separate new window for you to work on. In the scripts area, type in the following lines of code;

print("Loop starting!")

for i in range (10):

In the above lines of code, the first line works exactly in the same way as demonstrated in the Print("Good Morning") example. However, the second line is rather interesting. This line initiates a definite loop sequence, with the defined limit being set by the range followed by the desired integer. The i is the loop counter which will count the number of times the program loops, in this case, it will count upwards till nine because the stop instruction is the number 10, as soon as the 9th loop is completed, the loop will exit. Also, look at the colon ":" at the end of the line. This tells the computer that the following lines of code are actually a part of the loop.

Moreover, in Scratch, we saw that the instruction which is to be added into the loop function could be placed on the loop block directly. But in Python, we indent the instruction code by using a colon (":"). An indentation is characterized by four blank spaces left at the beginning of the new line; the IDE application does this automatically as soon as you press ENTER after an indentation.

```
print("Loop starting!")
```

```
for i in range (10):
```

```
print("Loop number", i)
```

This indentation is what allows python to differentiate between instructions that are not included in the loop and instructions, which are to be included in the loop (this indented code is known as being nested).

All the lines following this indentation will automatically contain four blank spaces because Thonny assumes that the following lines of code will also be the part of the loop. This will keep happening until you have written all the instructions which are part of the loop. To close the indentation, simply make a new indented blank line and press BACKSPACE, this will return the line to normal. Now, close the indentation as described and write the following line of code.

```
print("Loop finished!")
```

The sequence of the lines of code should be something like this;

```
print("Loop starting!")
```

```
for i in range (10):
```

print("Loop number", i)

print("Loop finished!")

In this program, the first line and last line is outside of the loop because they are not indented. The second line is where the loop starts and contains the indentation, whereas the third line is part of the loop.

Let's save this program as "indentation" and run the program. In the shell area, we will see the following output;

Loop starting!
Loop number 0
Loop number 1
Loop number 2
Loop number 3
Loop number 4
Loop number 5
Loop number 6
Loop number 7
Loop number 8
Loop number 9
Loop finished!

The reason why Python counts from zero instead of one is that Python is designed as a zero-indexed language. This means that it considers 0 as the beginning integer rather than 1. You can change this behavior by specifying the range instruction to be a range (1, 11) instead of range(10). With this, the loop will start counting from 1 to 10. You can do this for any number you want.

Just as how we used definite and indefinite loops in Scratch, the same can be done in Python. To use indefinite loops (loops that run forever), all you need to do is edit the 2nd line of code in the above program.

```
print("Loop starting!")

While True:

print("Loop running!")

print("Loop finished!")
```

You have now created an indefinite loop. This is because the end condition of the loop has not been specified as each time the message "loop running!" is printed, the program directs the code execution back to the start, and the whole process is repeated until the program itself is terminated. Save the program and run it to see the output in the shell area.

To terminate the program, simply click the red 'Stop' icon. The program will terminate without ever being able to reach the last line of the code.

Using conditionals and variables

Open up a new project by clicking the 'New' icon and in the scripts area, input the following line of code

```
userName = input ("What is your name? ")
```

Save the program and run it. The output of this program is that it displays a message asking for your name. After the end of the message, left-click the empty space, write a name, and hit ENTER. Nothing will happen in the program, but if you shift your focus to the right towards the variables window, you'll see that a variable 'userName' assigned with the value you just entered has been created.

To demonstrate how to use variables in python, we will pair the 'userName' variable with a conditional statement. In this demonstration, the program will ask us for our name, and based on our answer; it will give us a specific response.

if userName == "Clark Kent":

print("You are Superman!")

else:

print("You are not Superman!")

Now run the program after saving it and notice the output. In the first scenario, when the program asks us for our name, it compares it with the variable's value "Calrk Kent" to see if it matches. If our name matches the one in the variable, then the condition is said to be True; if it does not match, then the condition is said to be False. Depending on the result being True or False, the conditional statement instructs the program to execute one of the following lines of code.

Also, notice that instead of one equality "=" symbol, we used a double equality symbol "==." This is because a single equality symbol assigns a value to a variable, or in simpler terms, makes this value equal to this variable. While the double equality symbol makes a direct comparison. One is an assigning operator, while the other is a comparative operator.

Also, a text in quotation marks is referred to as a String. A number with or without quotation marks is referred to as an Integer. When you are combining two different types of information, for example, the text "How old are you?" with the reply 22, you will have to convert the integer into a string before they can be joined.

When working with numbers, you can also use the greater than '>' and lesser than '<' comparative operators. But to use the equal to operator, you'll have to use '==.' Similarly, equal to or greater than '=>' and equal to or less than '=<' can also be used.

We will now use some comparison operators in the loop example we used before.

while userName != "Clark Kent":

print("You are not Superman – try again!")

userName = input ("what is your name")

print("You are Superman!)

Upon running this program, you'll see that instead of quitting the program after telling you that you are not superman, it will keep inquiring your name until it is confirmed that you are indeed the superhero Superman.

Chapter 8

Raspberry PI Models

Model A/B

The very first line of Raspberry Pi models was known as the Model A and the Model B (as shown in the image above). Both models had the Broadcom BCM 2835 SoC within them, but had different specifications: Model A, for instance, had 256 MB of RAM, one USB port, and zero networking qualities; Model B had either a 256 MB or 512 MB of RAM depending on the date of the purchase, a 10/100 wired network port, and two USB ports.

These models were distinguishable because of their smaller than usual GPIO port, which has only 26 pins where is the larger, more advanced one has 40 pins. Both models also possess a full-size SD card storage instead of the compact microSD cards that the newer models come with. Although there are no longer manufactured, both the Model A and B are still compatible with most of the software that's designed for the newer models, except they don't use add-on hardware based on the HAT standard.

Model A+/B+

The original models proved to be very popular, but more than swiftly replaced with a new board design called the Plus. These later model iterations came with the 40-pin GPIO header while improving some of the other features. However, they didn't deviate from the BCM 2835 SoC, which means that there was not much of a difference in performance between the Plus models and the older models.

The hardware difference between the Model A+ and Model B+ is similar to the previous Model A and Model B: the A+ model, which has a smaller footprint than the A Model, either has a 256 or 512 MB of memory depending on the launch of the product, zero network capabilities, and a single USB port; the Model B+ has a 512 MB of memory, a 10/100 wired network port, and four USB ports. A+ and B+ are quite compatible with each software and device mentioned in this guide and have identical GPIO layouts as the newer models these days. If you have either of these models, the only reason you should upgrade is to gain additional memory, enjoyed built-in wireless capabilities, or improve performance.

Raspberry Pi 2

Whereas the Plus end previous other boards use the same BCM 2835 SoC processor, the newer Raspberry Pi 2 uses the new BCM 2836 SoC processor. Instead of one core like the original, the new processor features over four cores as well as 4 to 8 times the performance of the original – which makes everything from word processing to compiling code a much faster process. This new version also contains over 1GB (1024 MB) of RAM, doubling what was available for the previous one, which made memory-intensive applications and multitasking go much smoother and a lot more responsive.

When it comes to layout, not much has changed from the Model B+. For instance, the Raspberry Pi 2 has the same four USB ports, 40-pin GPIO header, 10/100 wired network ports as well as other ports. If you indeed have an add-on device or a case that works with the Model B+, it will work well with the Raspberry Pi 2 – only faster.

The new board comes with bigger software compatibility than the previous versions: even the proprietary operating system, Raspbian, can run operating systems such as Windows 10 IoT Core and Ubuntu that wasn't made available for the Raspberry Pi's predecessors.

Raspberry Pi 3

The last model before the fourth iteration, the Raspberry Pi 3, came with a newer processor at the time: the Broadcom BCM 2837. Being the 64-bit processor, not 32-bit, the new processor was considerably faster than the BCM 2836 found in the Raspberry Pi 2 version, which at the time was a massive upgrade from the BCM 2835 of the original and the Plus series. The Raspberry Pi 3 was also the first model to get built-in wireless support, which included a radio that connected to 2.4 GHz Wi-Fi networks and Bluetooth devices.

Like Pi 2, nothing much was changed with the layout: you would get the same four USB ports, 40-pin GPIO header, 10/100 wired network port, and several other ports that came with the last models. The only minor change comes with how the board interacts with specific add-on hardware, so if you're sure about whether a device is compatible with the Pi 3 model, then you should contact the vendor or manufacturer before buying to ensure that the software factored in that change.

One great advantage of the new Pi 3, other than the built-in wireless features and, of course, the improved performance, is its 64-bit processor. Switching over to this model given its new processor means that you will have better software compatibility performance and security over the 32-bit version of the previous models.

Raspberry Pi Zero

The Raspberry Pi Zero is by far not only the smallest board in the entire Raspberry Pi family, but it's also the cheapest of them all. Despite being the size of a couple of sticks of chewing gum that are stacked on top of each other, the Raspberry Pi Zero hardly lacks what the other models too: it has the same BCM 2835 SoC as well as 512 MB of RAM like the Raspberry Pi Model B+, and runs in a slightly faster speed for better performance.

However, Pi Zero needs the aid of certain caveats when it comes to using. For example, the mini-HDMI port and single micro-USB port require adapters before they can be connected to standard peripherals; there's no DSI port; the 3.5 mm AV jack is gone, the CSI port needs an adapter; and while it's present, the GPIO header needs pins that have to be purchased and soldered into place before it can be used.

We don't recommend the Pi Zero if you're a beginner. But if you are a more experienced user and want to bring more intelligence to embedded projects – especially when you experience troubles with cost, power draw, and size – the Pi Zero is the board you need to get your hands on.

The Raspberry Pi 4 Model B

Now, we were going to look into the latest Raspberry Pi 4 Model B, see what it's made of and how you can make it work. Although it seems like a lot is going into this tiny board, we assure you that the Raspberry Pi board is quite easy to understand - especially its components.

One of the most critical components is the *system-on-chip* (SoC), which is the centerpiece covered in a metal cap. It is called system-on-chip as there is a silicon chip underneath the metal cover if you pry it open. This chip is also known as an integrated circuit that contains most of the Raspberry Pi's operating system. Some of the most critical aspects contained within the chip are the graphics processing unit (GPU), handles the visual side of things, and the central processing unit (CPU), also known as the brain of a computer.

But without memory, the CPU would be of no use. But if you were to look to the side of the SoC, you'll find another small, black, plastic square chip (as the image shows), which is the board's random-access memory (RAM). This RAM, when in use, holds whatever you're doing and will write it to the microSD card when you save your work. To reiterate from what we said earlier, the RAM is volatile, which means when the Pi board is powered off, you lose your data. On the other hand, the microSD card is non-volatile, and if you save your data in it, you won't be able to lose it even when the power is out.

Then at the top left a corner of the board. You'll come across another silver lid which covers the radio, which is what gives the Raspberry Pi its ability to connect with other devices wirelessly. The radio behaves as two separate components: a Wi-Fi radio that wirelessly connects to other computer networks; and the Bluetooth radio that connects to peripherals like keyboards and mice or for sending or receiving data from nearby smart devices such as sensors or smartphones.

Then there's the USB controller represented by a black, plastic-covered chip that's at the bottom edge of the board just behind the middle set of USB ports. This component is responsible for running all four of the USB ports. There's the even smaller network controller chip that handles the board's Ethernet network ports. And then finally the smallest black chip that's a little over the USB Type-C power connector that's located to the board's upper left side, known as the power management integrated circuit (PMIC). This chip is responsible for turning the micro USB port power into the power that the Raspberry Pi requires to run.

Conclusion

Thank you for reading this book. The next step is to use the information that you have learned in this book and get to coding with Raspberry Pi. You are going to be able to create a lot of projects that are going to improve your life so that it is more comfortable.

The Raspberry Pi is indeed a technological marvel, and it will always be surprised as to what this tiny machine is capable of. Not only does this little monster pack a punch in terms of power and capability, but the Raspberry Pi is also in a league of its own with regards to its adaptability to an entire array of possible applications. Just as how the Raspberry Pi's usefulness knows no limits and has no defined boundary, we could only learn so much in this beginner's level book. There's still an entire island's worth of knowledge to still explore regarding the Pi and its capability and how we can use it to the best of its abilities. However, this book has addressed all of the essential concepts to their basic form so that the reader will be able to tackle any problem he comes across if he wants to use the

Raspberry Pi as a pocket computer or as a project piece.

Be humble in the way that you approach everything. Don't be afraid to admit that you're wrong or that you aren't as capable as what you want to think and ask for help on one of the communities. The Raspberry Pi is altogether one of the coolest pieces of technology out there right now, and it can do so much. Still, it can also be frustrating to the programmer because it can do exactly as much as the programmer can make it do.

The Raspberry Pi is indeed a wonderful device. It's small and handy so that you can carry it with you anywhere. It is very affordable and widely accessible, so you can easily purchase a dozen without breaking your budget. You can never have too many Raspberry Pi devices for your projects.

If you want to hone your skills, unleash your creative side, and create things that are useful and unique, you should keep working and practicing. Remember that you can get tips and advice, as well as share your ideas with other Raspberry Pi users. You may even form friendships from the online community.

The affordability and accessibility of the Raspberry Pi can help you work on multiple projects. If you made a mistake, you could try again. You can even patent and sell your work. From simple devices, you can come up with tools that the whole world can benefit from. The opportunities are limitless, and you can reach for your dreams with the help of the Raspberry Pi.

Rather than pass the time watching TV, checking your social media, or mindlessly surfing the Internet, you can be productive and use the Raspberry Pi to experiment with projects.

The Raspberry Pi is truly one of the greatest inventions today. With such a tiny device, great things can be achieved.

Top-notch programmers don't give up along the way. Go ahead and practice to conceptualize all the ideas you have learned in this book.

Remember, the rule of thumb in learning - Raspberry Pi included - is practice; and undoubtedly: Good practice makes perfect.

I wish you the very best of luck!